A Journey To Find Rhyme After Sexual Abuse

TAMMY KENNEDY, MS

Illustrated by Kyle Miller and Mike Dillard

Copyright © 2016 Tammy Kennedy
All rights reserved.

All characters in this story, including *Lil' J™*, *King of Music™*, *DJ Rap-a-Lot™*, *Jazzy Jazz™*, *Lie Monsters™*, *MC ShameR™*, *Icky Ick™*, *Guil-T™*, and *Con the Artist™* are trademarks of Tammy Kennedy. This is a work of fiction. All characters appearing in this work are fictitious. Any resemblance to real persons, living or dead, is purely coincidental.

ISBN: 978-0-9910841-4-2

King's Treasure Box Ministries, Cumming, GA
The King's Treasure Box Ministries (KTBM) is a 501 (C)3 non-profit, tax-exempt organization.

Illustrated by: Kyle Miller (Chapter 1-2) and Mike Dillard (Chapters 3-8)

Art Direction and Design: Steven Tyrrell / tyrrellcreative.com

Dedicated to Debra Goldstone

My Debba. Why do I love, appreciate, and owe you so much: "love to the moon," "if I were a rich man," dishwasher fairy, Grammy's 10 raisins or was it 12, floss, spinach and balsamic, "I'll never grow up—not me," hospitality, white robe, buy-in, THM or junk, and, of course, worship? I wonder if Lil' J would exist if your hand and my foot had not connected under the table that night many years ago. I can say with 100% certainty that I would not be the "me" I am without the influence of you in my life. You are so woven into the fabric of the tapestry of your "Tam." You are one of the very best people I know and you will always be "In the top 5!"

TABLE OF CONTENTS

Preface	How To Use This Book	i
Chapter 1	Lil' J Loved Music	1
Chapter 2	Lil' J Lost His Rhyme	13
Chapter 3	Believing Lies	27
Chapter 4	Liar MC ShameR Says, "You're Bad"	35
Chapter 5	Liar Guil-T Says, "It's Your Fault"	51
Chapter 6	Liar Icky Ick Says, "You're Messed Up n' Dirty"	65
Chapter 7	Con the Artist Says, "You've Got a RIGHT to Rage!"	81
Chapter 8	Lil' J Puts It All Together	93

PREFACE

HOW TO USE THIS BOOK

Your special assignment to help your Lil' Warrior:

This book was written for boys ages 6 – 12 who have experienced sexual abuse. First read the book from cover-to-cover on your own to determine whether or not you can handle the material. You will also want to begin building your own support network fast. **This book is not meant to help you be the therapist**. Your child just needs you to be supportive and to listen.

Before you begin, tell him you found a storybook that has helped other kids. Reassure him, let him know you love him, you believe him, and want to help him with the pain. Let him know that parts of this special book will be fun and that you are going on an adventure together to help Lil' J fight some monsters.

GET CREATIVE – The Lie chapters, where you will spend most of your time, are the most important. As someone who loves and knows him best, you will be highly effective in helping him challenge his beliefs about the abuse. Talk about the lies Lil' J believes throughout the story. Use the Lie Monsters as a tool to help your warrior sort out truth from lies. DJ Rap-a-Lot and Jazzy Jazz will be there to help guide the dialogue. Together you will help Lil' J fight the Lie Monsters who come to tell him that the abuse was his fault, that he is bad, and that he is now dirty. You will be great lie detectives.

NOTE: If you are a survivor of sexual abuse and have not dealt with your own brokenness, I strongly urge you to get help now! You cannot walk him through this process as effectively without support and healing yourself. You may be struggling with believing the same lies your child believes. I care about you, too!

This will be a hard journey for your family, but many treasures can come from pain. Get all the help you can afford and fight to get even more. You need the support and so does he. My purpose here is to empower parents or safe loved ones to know how to talk with their child about what happened without causing more damage. Even the most wonderful parents often do not know how to handle this topic.

CHAPTER 1

Lil' J was a very happy kid with big bright eyes and a huge smile. He loved his toys, but he loved music even more, especially rap. Lil' J didn't talk until he was two, but when he began to sing at ten months old, his sweet face lit up so brightly that any audience would need shades to handle his shine.

ONE DAY, LIL' J'S MOTHER GAVE HIM A GIFT, A VERY SPECIAL CAP FOR A VERY EXTRAORDINARY KID!

Lil' J and his talent grew. He was always beaming with a smile, especially on the mornings he woke up to the smell of pancakes. Sometimes Lil' J's dad poured extra syrup when his mom wasn't looking. Lil' J and his dad created lyrics in stacks about anything, even raps about flapjacks!

Sadly, everything changed when Lil' J was about five years old. That's when his dad lost his job and his parents started arguing all the time. Hot pancakes were replaced by cold cereal all alone.

Lil' J thought, *SOMEDAY I'LL MAKE SO MUCH MONEY WITH MY MUSIC THAT THEY WON'T FIGHT*

ANYMORE.

On the night of his sixth birthday, Lil' J was supposed to have a party, but his parents got into a huge and very loud fight. His mom started crying and sent Lil' J to his room. Later, his dad

came in holding a suitcase to say, "Goodbye." It was a very bad, yucky, awful kind of day.

Days turned into weeks as Lil'J waited and waited for his dad to return home. He never did. Lil' J's life was changing suddenly, but he tried to be brave.

"Honey, you need to start going to the recreation center after school now," his mom said.

"Why?" Lil' J asked.

"You know I have to work two jobs," she said. "And you're too young to stay home alone."

The first few days were very hard because Lil' J didn't know anyone. He reminded himself, ***I CAN'T CRY. I'M THE MAN OF THE HOUSE NOW; I'VE GOT TO TAKE CARE OF MY MOM.***

At the end of the first week, Lil' J was dribbling the basketball, when a man walked up and introduced himself as Mr. Links, a retired music teacher who worked at the center. Mr. Links was very friendly and even asked Lil' J if he had any music talents. Lil' J performed a rap and before he knew it, the kids were clapping!

From that day forward, Lil' J could hardly wait for his school day to end. He loved practicing his rap skills with Mr. Links while the other kids watched. Most every day Lil' J and Mr. Links spent time working on a new beat.

Lil' J said, **"MR. LINKS, I WANT TO BE A FAMOUS RAPPER SOMEDAY. I ALSO WANT TO BE A FAMOUS DRUMMER AND MAYBE EVEN A JAZZ MUSICIAN."**

"Sounds like if it has to do with music you want to learn everything about everything!" said Mr. Links.

"YES! AND I WANT TO BE THE BEST!" Lil' J grinned. He wrote lyrics all day in his head. He could feel the beat and music in his body and soul. Lil' J was most happy when he was performing for his classmates and his favorite teacher, Mrs. Witkin.

"You crack me up, Lil' J!" Mrs. Witkin would say. She was especially

"LOOKIN' CRAZY COOL, MUSIC MAKES THE RULES. HIP HOP HOORAY, PLAYIN' HARDER IN MY J'S. BANGIN' OUT MY SOUND, BRINGIN' TALENT TO MY TOWN. LAUGHIN' WITH MY RHYMES, KEEPING UP WITH DA TIMES. RIDIN' ON THIS BEAT, TURNING UP DA HEAT."

 kind to him and he loved to make her laugh.

Most days, before heading over to the rec center, Lil' J stayed behind to chat with Mrs. Witkin. Over time, he began telling her about some of the pain he felt about his parents fighting and his father leaving.

At the rec center, Mr. Links always gave Lil' J extra attention. "Boy, you've got music in your bones!" said Mr. Links. "And you're pretty good with that ball!"

Lil' J loved basketball almost as much as his rhyme.

CHAPTER 2

LIL' J LOST HIS RHYME

One afternoon, Mr. Links pulled Lil' J aside and said, "I've got a surprise for you in the basement."

Lil' J was super excited when he saw the old drum set! He ran to hug Mr. Links and said, "I'm gonna play so good, create crazy beats, and make you so proud that you'll never leave me!"

Mr. Links hugged Lil' J really tight, like he'd never let go. Lil' J tried to ignore the uneasy feeling in his gut and just be thankful that Mr. Links loved him so much.

Unlike with the other kids, Mr. Links began giving Lil' J private drum lessons.

"Our close friendship needs to be a secret," said Mr. Links. "The other kids will be jealous." As

he stood behind Lil' J to massage his shoulders, he said, "All good musicians need help relaxing."

To avoid some of the touching, Lil' J learned to race straight to the drums and begin playing. Sometimes the massages felt good, but mostly they felt awful.

Some days Lil' J lied. "My stomach hurts. I can't have lessons today." On those days, Mr. Links made Lil' J do his homework instead of letting him play basketball with his friends. Lil' J loved basketball and hated homework, but sometimes avoiding the lessons was worth missing basketball. Lil' J felt angry that Mr. Links didn't make the other kids do homework before they could play.

For many weeks, Lil' J and Mr. Links spent time downstairs for drum lessons. Lil' J tried to avoid the massages, but Mr. Links said things like, "You must not appreciate all I'm trying to do for you. Having tight muscles will affect your music." Or he sometimes said, "If you don't want to do the things we need to do, I'm sure one of the other kids would love to be in your place."

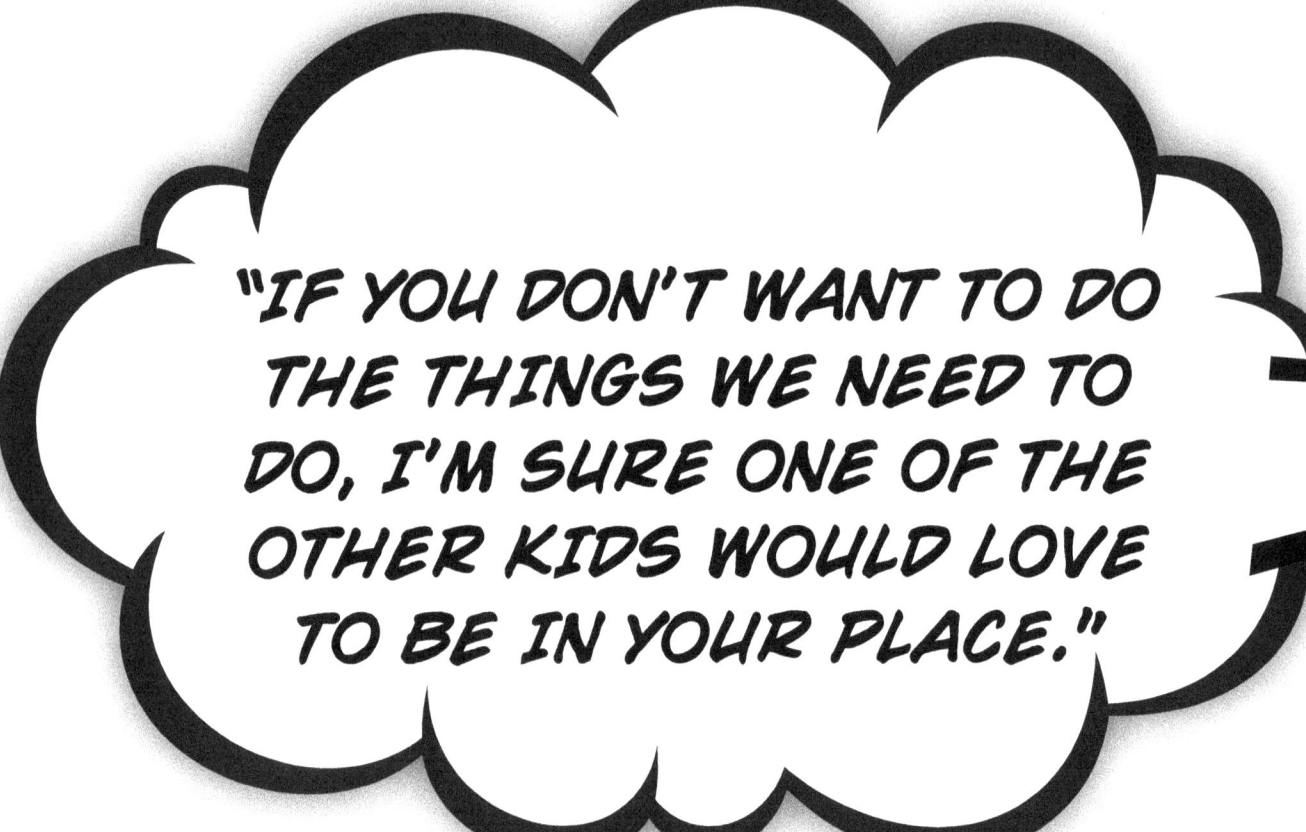

"IF YOU DON'T WANT TO DO THE THINGS WE NEED TO DO, I'M SURE ONE OF THE OTHER KIDS WOULD LOVE TO BE IN YOUR PLACE."

A few months later, Mr. Links surprised Lil' J by handing him a saxophone. Mr. Links said, "What we're doing is right because we love each other." Then the touching got even worse!

Lil' J listened to what Mr. Links was saying about keeping everything a secret, but his mind was going crazy. His heart was racing. He wanted to run and hide. He wanted to scream at Mr. Links, but his mouth stayed shut. Lil' J was too scared and too confused to move even a muscle.

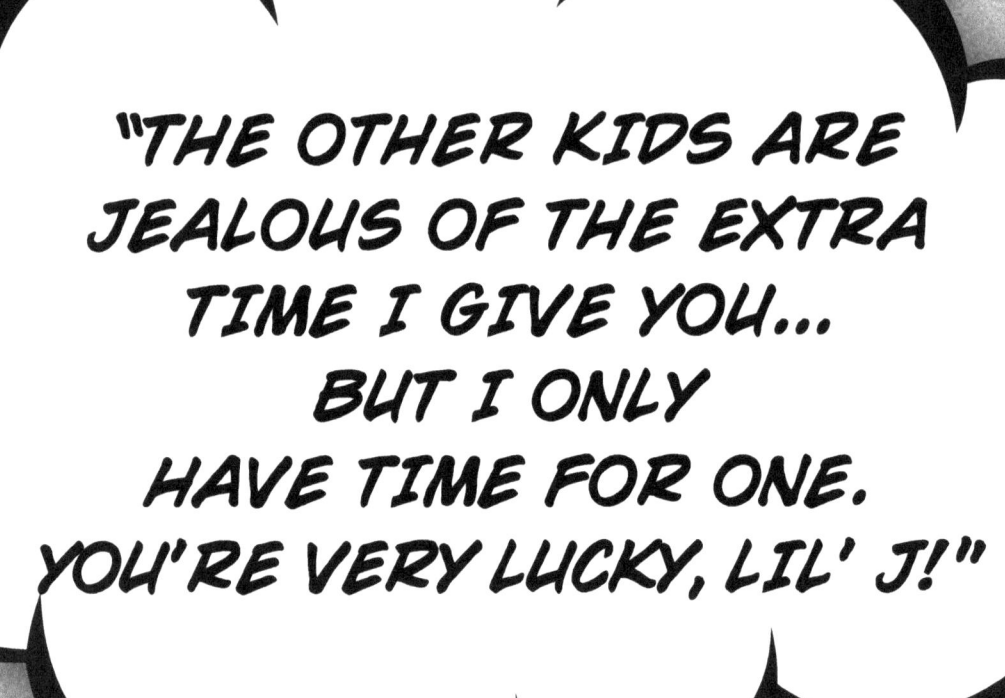

"THE OTHER KIDS ARE JEALOUS OF THE EXTRA TIME I GIVE YOU... BUT I ONLY HAVE TIME FOR ONE. YOU'RE VERY LUCKY, LIL' J!"

Lil' J loved when Mr. Links said things like, "Lil' J, you're the most talented nine-year-old I've ever met. Son, you were born to play!"

Since his dad left, Lil' J had missed feeling special. Though Lil' J loved learning to play the new instruments and performing for his friends, the guilt and embarrassment he felt was overwhelming.

Mr. Links told him, "The other kids are jealous of the extra time I give you. They beg me to be their music

coach, but I only have time for one. You're very lucky Lil' J. You're the only one with enough talent to be famous one day."

Lil' J tried to focus on the future. If I become a famous musician someday, Mom won't have to work so hard. She'll be happy, and then Dad will come back home. It was money that caused the fights, so if I become rich, everything will be perfect. What Lil' J wanted most was for his family to be proud of him. Mr. Links was doing so many nice things for Lil' J, but also doing so many wrong things! His biggest secret, what Lil' J felt the most shame about, was that sometimes it felt...good. He couldn't explain the anger he felt, the self-hate, the embarrassment, and the ocean-sized guilt. This secret made Lil' J feel so lonely and confused.

After about a year of drum lessons, then a year of saxophone lessons, Mr. Links announced he had another surprise. As they descended down into what was now

being called Lil' J's private music studio, the click Lil' J heard when Mr. Links closed the door caused waves of panic. Smiling as he turned around, Mr. Links handed a new shiny guitar to Lil' J, who was stunned. The locked door, the new gift, the smile, the . . .

Lil' J knew what was coming. As he accepted the heavy new guitar, time seemed to stand still. He tried to quickly come up with some of his favorite rhymes to stop

"LOST THE RHYME IN MY HEAD;
MUSIC FEELING DEAD.
MIND RAGIN' IN A WAR;
DEEP DESIRE TO EVEN THE SCORE.
FEELIN' CAPTIVE LIKE IN JAIL;
PAIN TOO DEEP TO EVEN TELL.

NEVER BE THE SAME, KNOWIN'
I'M THE ONE TO BLAME.
I'M TRAPPED IN TIME;
GOD I NEED A SIGN!"

the fear, the rage, and especially the guilt, but those lyrics were lost. Instead, a very different sort of rhyme came to Lil' J's mind that day. It now seemed all the original music in his soul had finally escaped, and what was left sounded nothing like his beat.

Lil' J's lyrics were new and unfamiliar, but he recognized the feelings. As Mr. Links put his hand on Lil' J's shoulder, for the first time ever, the rhyme in Lil' J's heart and mind stopped. Even his new rage song was nowhere to be found. He could see himself on stage as he had a million times before, but at that moment, his mind was blank. He imagined holding the microphone to his lips, but there were no words, no thoughts, no music, only noise.

LIL' J LOST ALL HIS RHYME THAT DAY!

CHAPTER 3

Yes, Lil' J lost all his rhyme that day. He rarely wore his favorite cap anymore, the one his mom gave him. Lil' J didn't feel he deserved anything special. In fact, out of pain and desperation, he did something new.

HE ASKED THE KING OF MUSIC FOR A SIGN.

As Lil' J walked home, something amazing happened. While listening to his music, he heard something he had never heard before.

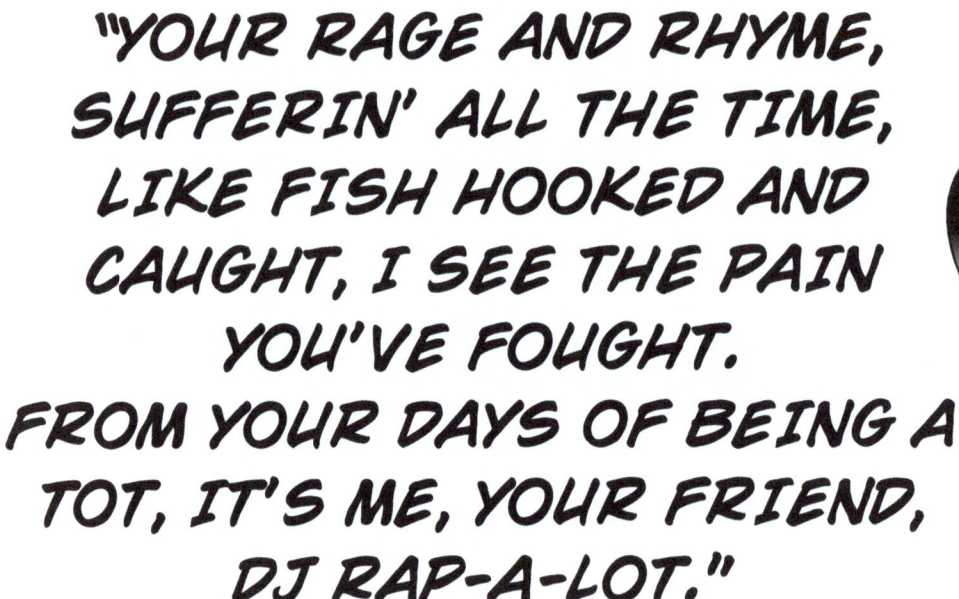

"YOUR RAGE AND RHYME, SUFFERIN' ALL THE TIME, LIKE FISH HOOKED AND CAUGHT, I SEE THE PAIN YOU'VE FOUGHT.
FROM YOUR DAYS OF BEING A TOT, IT'S ME, YOUR FRIEND, DJ RAP-A-LOT."

Suddenly his phone shook, light gleamed from all sides, and before he knew it, DJ Rap-a-Lot appeared before him, spinning some new tracks with an amazing sound. Lil' J thought he'd gone crazy when he heard…

"YOU ASKED THE KING FOR A SIGN. HE SENT ME WITH THE RHYME. HE SEES YOUR PAIN; YOU'RE NOT THE ONE TO BLAME. HE'S GONNA SEE YA THROUGH. CHECK OUT WHAT THE KING OF MUSIC CAN DO."

Could there really be a King of Music, and did someone really care? As this thought crossed Lil' J's mind, DJ Rap-a-Lot said, "Lil' J, you're valuable, and the King of Music is proud of you. You really are a great musician, just like He created you to be."

Lil' J said, "You don't understand! I used to be a good musician, but I lost it all. I can't rhyme anymore, and I don't care. It's all stupid anyway."

DJ Rap-a-Lot said, "The problem, Lil' guy, is that you're believin' a lot of lies! Your music will come back when you download the truth. The King of Music has an enemy known as Master Deceiver, who wants to steal every good plan the King has for His children. Master Deceiver has waged a war against you and has sent four Lie Monsters to destroy you: MC ShameR, Guil-T, Icky Ick, and Con the Artist.

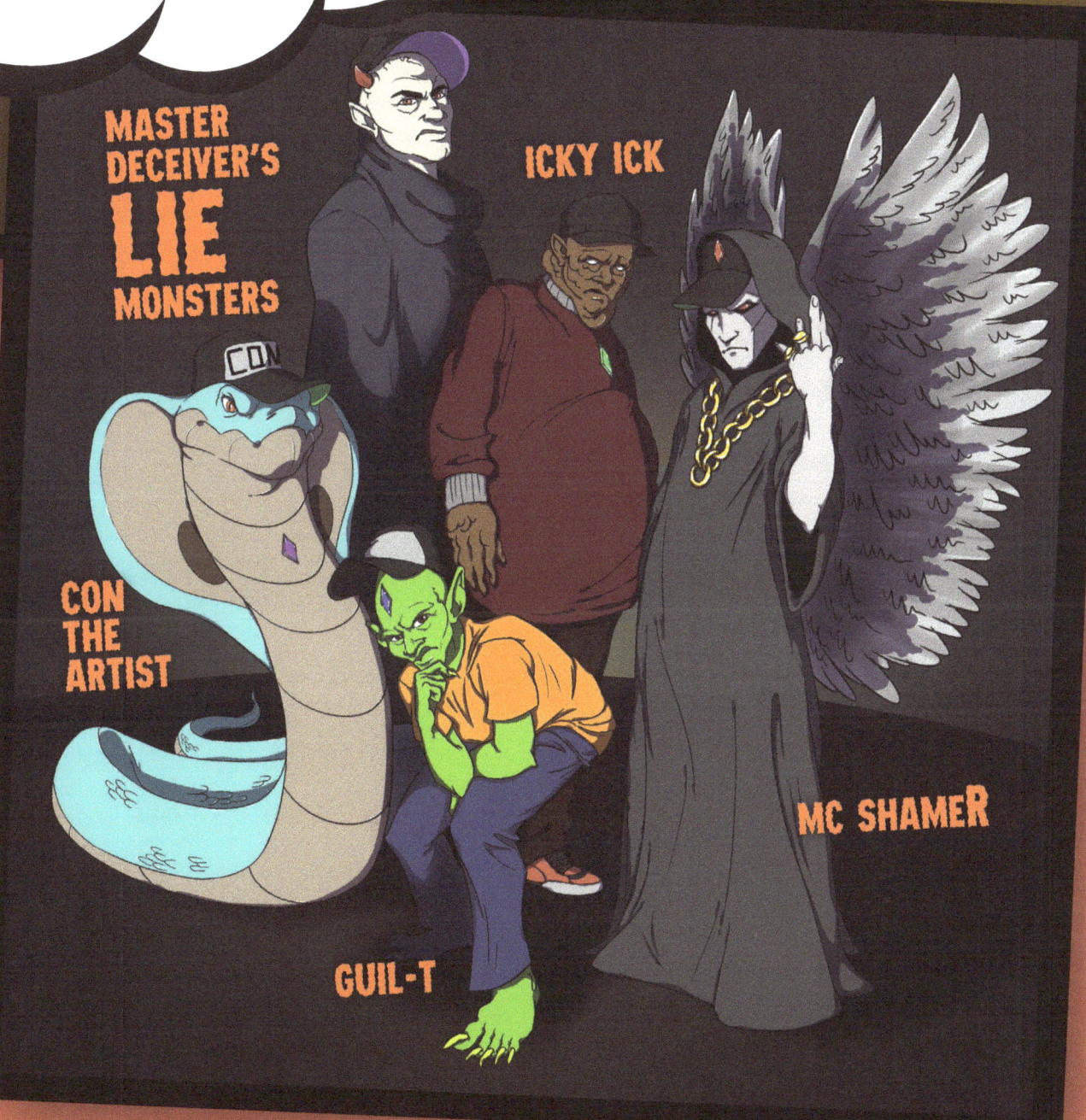

THE COLORED STONE ON EACH MONSTER HOLDS THE POWER TO DECEIVE YOU.

The Lie Monsters' job is to steal our music, our song, our rap, and even our life. Let's fight all these liars so you can feel the music again."

CHAPTER 4

LIAR MC SHAMER SAYS, "YOU'RE BAD"

A brief moment of hope began to seep into Lil' J's heart, until he heard MC ShameR, the liar, drop this mean beat.

Lil' J heard MC ShameR's rhyme, and it sounded like truth to his hurting soul. Knowing what Lil' J was believing, DJ Rap-a-Lot broke through and dropped the King's beat.

"MC SHAMER, YOU'RE SUCH A LIAR.
SHUT UP, CUZ LIL' J'S ON FIRE.
WANTING SOMEONE TO CARE,
KNOWING THE WORLD IS NEVER FAIR,
NEEDING LOVE CAN HURT SO BAD,
A FATHER LEAVING MAKES ANYONE SAD.
MR. LINKS DID TERRIBLE THINGS;
HE STOLE YOUR RHYME
AND DESIRE TO SING.
MC SHAMER, CRUEL AND WICKED,
LISTENING TO THE KING'LL
BE YOUR TICKET.
HE RESPECTS YOU AND CAN HEAL.
HE TRULY CARES ABOUT THE
PAIN YOU FEEL."

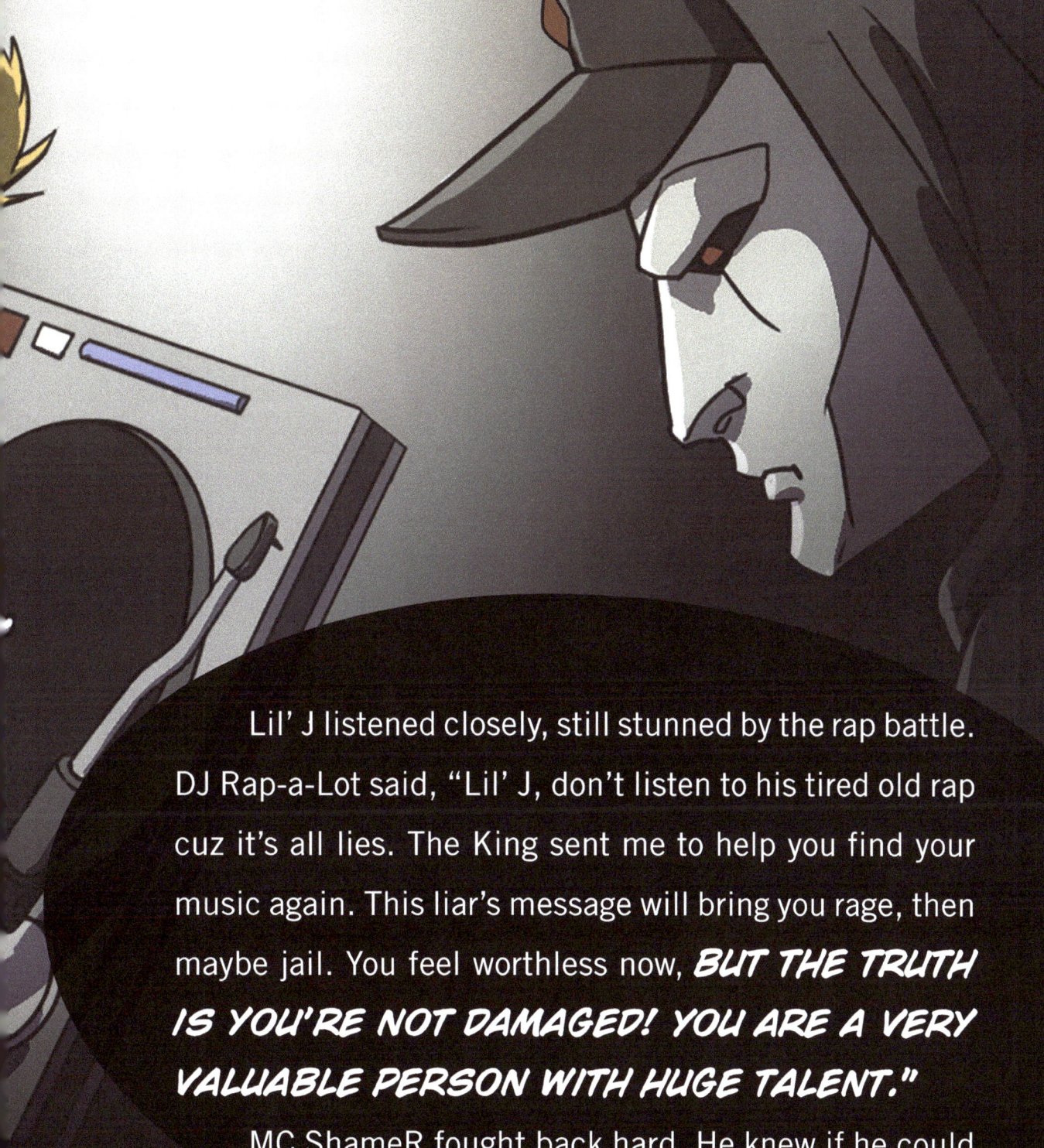

Lil' J listened closely, still stunned by the rap battle. DJ Rap-a-Lot said, "Lil' J, don't listen to his tired old rap cuz it's all lies. The King sent me to help you find your music again. This liar's message will bring you rage, then maybe jail. You feel worthless now, **BUT THE TRUTH IS YOU'RE NOT DAMAGED! YOU ARE A VERY VALUABLE PERSON WITH HUGE TALENT."**

MC ShameR fought back hard. He knew if he could make Lil' J keep his memories and pain a secret, he could control Lil' J and take all his power. Using Lil' J's own voice, MC ShameR whispered…

"DON'T TELL CUZ PAIN WASN'T THAT BAD;
TIME TO STOP BLAMING THE DEADBEAT DAD.
TRUTH BE TOLD, GUYS AREN'T VICTIMS;
KNOWING SOMEWHERE THAT WAS WRITTEN.
ON THOSE DAYS, IF I'D BEEN BRAVE,
I'D HAVE FOUGHT; HE'D NEVER HAVE HIS WAY.
HIDE THE HURT AND THE PAIN;
ACT AS IF I'M COOL AND SANE.
WISHING TO BE TOTALLY FREE, KNOWING THE TRUTH THAT SOMETHING'S WRONG WITH ME."

DJ Rap-a-Lot knew Lil' J's heart and said, "Lil' man, we are all made to need love and respect. When that doesn't happen, it leaves a hole in our soul, and we work hard to fill it. Your father left, and your mother has two jobs.

MR. LINKS HAS BEEN DOING TERRIBLE THINGS TO YOU. HE TRICKED YOU BY GIVING YOU TIME, ATTENTION, PRAISE, AND EVEN GIFTS FOR THE WRONG REASONS. HE WAS USING YOU. THIS IS WHAT UNSAFE PEOPLE DO."

Lil' J wanted to believe DJ Rap-a-Lot, but felt ashamed. He loved the music and spending time with someone he thought was his friend. Lil' J hated most of the touching but had been afraid to say, "No!"

He felt angry and hated to admit his fear because he thought being scared meant he was a wimp.

Lil' J wanted to believe him, but he had listened to the lies for so long...

"DON'T WANNA REMEMBER, WANT TO FORGET;
BREAKING OUT, IN A COLD COLD SWEAT.
YOU TELLING ME, THE ICKY FEELING INSIDE,
I DIDN'T EARN, SO I DON'T HAVE TO HIDE?
I WANT TO BELIEVE; I WANT TO BE FREE
ALL THESE FEELINGS, IMPRISONING ME.
KEEPING THE SECRET, WAS THAT MY PART?
NOW I SEE, IT'S HOW I LOST MY SPARK.
I FEEL ALONE AND OH SO SAD;
BUT YOU'RE TELLING ME, THAT I'M NOT BAD?
HIS ATTENTION KEPT ME IN LINE;

MAYBE THIS SHAME IS HIS AND NOT MINE?"

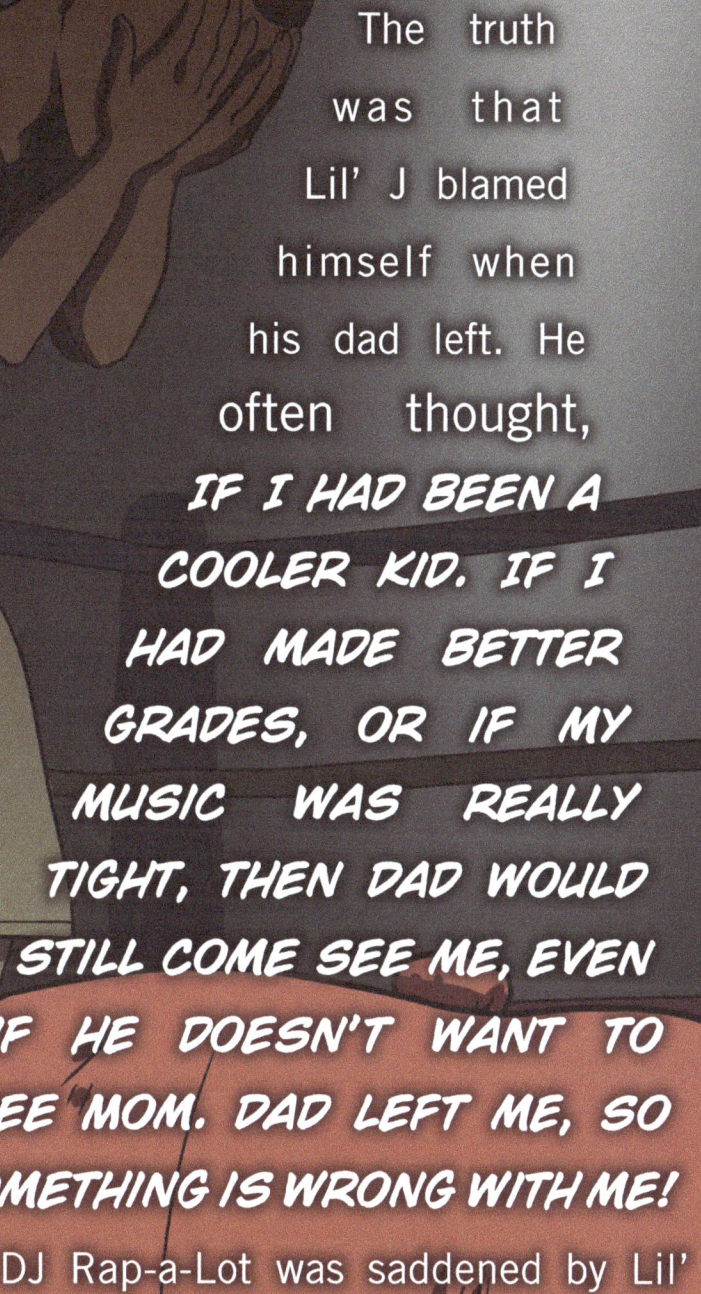

The truth was that Lil' J blamed himself when his dad left. He often thought, *IF I HAD BEEN A COOLER KID. IF I HAD MADE BETTER GRADES, OR IF MY MUSIC WAS REALLY TIGHT, THEN DAD WOULD STILL COME SEE ME, EVEN IF HE DOESN'T WANT TO SEE MOM. DAD LEFT ME, SO SOMETHING IS WRONG WITH ME!*

DJ Rap-a-Lot was saddened by Lil' J's pain. He knew there was power in the truth, which would bring Lil' J's music back. When DJ Rap-a-Lot began his tune, something awesome happened! Lil' J felt the words surrounding him, lifting him up, the truth lifting off the clouds of shame and defeat. DJ Rap-a-Lot continued...

"LIL' J, YOU'LL NEED TO FEEL;
IT'S SO VITAL IF YOU WANT TO HEAL.
YOU'LL NEED TIME, JUST TO MOURN;
LOTS OF PAIN, YOUR CHILDHOOD TORN.
KING'S PLAN, NOT JUST TO COPE;
HE SENT ME TO GIVE YOU HOPE.
YOU WERE BORN JUST TO SHINE; THE KING HAS ALWAYS CALLED YOU 'MINE.'
STRONG, BRAVE, WARRIOR, EASY TO LOVE;
YOU'RE A TALENT STRAIGHT FROM ABOVE.
EVEN THOUGH YOU'RE FAITHLESS NOW,
WE'RE GONNA HELP AND SHOW YOU HOW.
YOU GOT TALENT, YOU GOT RHYME, SO MUCH POSSIBILITY, JUST GIVE IT TIME."

MC ShameR was furious that Lil' J was beginning to believe the truth. He rushed at Lil' J and tried to knock him down, but Lil' J was ready. MC ShamerR was the one who ended up on the ground!

"I WON'T HIDE THOUGHTS OR FEELINGS.
I'LL SHARE MY PAIN TO BEGIN MY HEALING.
MC SHAMER'S SUCH A LIAR.
MY HOPE AND SONG LIFTS ME HIGHER AND HIGHER.
ONCE ASHAMED BUT NOW I SEE,
LINKS WAS WRONG
AND I'M SET FREE.
HE WAS ACTING OH SO NICE;
HE WAS FEEDING HIS OWN VICE.
NO MORE MASK TO HIDE BEHIND;
I SURVIVED AND BRIGHT
I'LL SHINE!

CHAPTER 5

As Lil' J began believing the truth, that he was talented, brave, and truly awesome, Master Deceiver got very angry, so he sent another liar to destroy Lil' J's music. This liar's name was Guil-T. He loved to make kids feel guilty, especially about things that were not their fault!

Lil' J felt guilty just about every minute of every day. If his mom was stressed about money, Lil' J felt guilty about needing school clothes. If his best friend was in a bad mood, Lil' J was sure it was his fault. He even blamed himself when his favorite team lost in the playoffs. Lil' J hadn't worn his special hat during the game.

One of Lil' J's guiltiest moments occurred at the rec center just before his tenth birthday. With seconds remaining, Lil' J got fouled and had to make a free throw. Before he could shoot, someone blurted out, "Hey, Music Boy, what do you and Links do all afternoon down in the basement?" The question seemed to hang in the air just like when the ball got stuck in the rim, and everyone just stared at it. The question caused vivid pictures that he couldn't delete to flash in Lil' J's mind. He didn't remember anything else.

The buzzer rang. He had missed the shot. They lost by one point! Lil' J was crushed. This was his fault, too!

The King of Music became very angry when Guil-T began pounding Lil' J with lies. Instead of pain, the King wants His children to be confident, enjoy their talents, make great music, and have fun. Nothing feels fun when you have Guil-T yelling in your head, telling you lies!

"LIL' J, YOU KNOW YOU'RE WRONG. YOU SIN AND SIN AND HAVE NO SONG."

He makes people want to keep secrets, and then we never learn the truth because we don't talk about our pain.

With the game over and seeing Lil' J's pain, DJ Rap-a-Lot stepped in. He knew Lil ' J needed some coaching.

*"LIL J, YOU WERE BORN TO SHINE;
KING OF MUSIC CALLS YOU 'MINE.'
LISTEN TO ME SPEAKING TRUTH;
SHAKE OFF THE GUILT,
ROOTED IN YOUR YOUTH.
LISTEN TO ME, LET GO OF BLAME.
SHAKE OFF THE GUILT,
SHAKE OFF THE SHAME."*

"Lil' J, Guil-T is cruel and sneaky. He's telling you lies night and day, so stop listening to his tired beat. Mr. Links started touching you when you were a small boy. He is the adult, and he knew it was wrong! Mr. Links often used the word 'we' and said 'feeling love' makes touching okay.

The TRUTH is you're a very talented and amazing kid! Most importantly, YOU DID NOTHING WRONG! Go fight with all your might!"

As Lil' J began believing DJ Rap-a-Lot, Guil-T broke through again.

"YOU'RE A BOY,
WANTING TO BE A MAN,
YOUR DESTRUCTION
MY FINAL PLAN.
HERE I AM, YOUR GUILT INSIDE;
HANG YO' HEAD, RUN AND HIDE.
YOU MUST BE PUNISHED FOR
WHAT YOU DID;
EVEN WHEN YOU'RE GROWN
AND NOT A KID.
I'LL RULE YOUR HEART,
MY NAME'S GUIL-T.
I'LL LOCK YOU UP,
YOU WON'T BE FREE."

Just as Guil-T said, "You won't be free," DJ Rap-a-Lot blasted the ugly liar and shut him up with this sound...

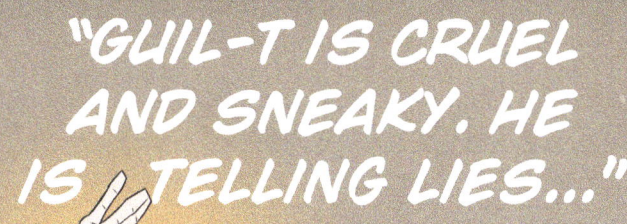

"YOU'LL LEARN TO LAUGH AND LEARN TO PLAY, CASTING CHAINS OF GUILT AWAY.
YOU CAN SAY, 'THE GUILT'S NOT MINE. HE'S THE ONE WHO DID THE CRIME.'
YOU CAN CHOOSE TO FIGHT AND SHINE; YOU CAN WORK TO FIND YOUR RHYME."

Lil' J replied, "But it is my fault. I kept going downstairs."

"Don't you remember acting sick, knowing this meant missing basketball with your friends?" asked DJ Rap-a-Lot. "The truth is, you wanted a friend. Mr. Links acted like he cared and wanted to help you, but that was a lie. He knew the way he touched you was wrong, and he knew how to trick you to keep everything a secret."

Lil' J dropped his head, but he was listening to every word.

DJ Rap-a-Lot continued. "Lil' J, you want to be a great musician and make your friends and family proud. There is nothing wrong with having those dreams. You are an amazing kid and the King of Music and I are very proud of you. Please believe me, you did nothing wrong!"

Lil' J considered his words and said,

"I WANNA BELIEVE; I WANNA FIGHT.
I'VE HEARD THE LIES;
THEY SEEM SO RIGHT.
HARD TO BELIEVE,
NOT ME THAT'S WRONG;

HARD TO BELIEVE,
I'LL GET BACK MY SONG.
PAIN SO BAD, WORSE THAN A KNIFE;
INNOCENCE LOST,
CAN I STILL HAVE A WIFE?
I'M REAL SCARED, BUT TRY I MUST;
LEARNING HOW, WHO CAN I TRUST?"

DJ Rap-a-Lot replied,

"TAKE A CHANCE AND BE PROUD;
SAY THE TRUTH AND SAY IT LOUD.
ERASE THE LIES,
AND FIGHT REAL STRONG. SAY,
'I'M GOOD AND WASN'T WRONG.'"

Hearing DJ's message and thinking about the lies he's believed, Lil' J sent this assault,

"GUIL-T, YOU'RE LOSIN' THIS BATTLE. YOU FELLOW LIARS, RUN OFF AN' TATTLE.

MASTER DECEIVER WON'T LIKE THIS. HE'S GONNA SHOUT, HE'S GONNA HISS.

I'M SAYIN' IT LOUD
AN SAYIN' IT CLEAR
I'M KICKING YOU OUT,
I'LL HAVE NO FEAR!
WANTING LOVE WAS NOT A CRIME.
KING OF MUSIC,
BRINGING BACK MY RHYME.
SHINING BRIGHT
AS EVER BEFORE,
LETTING THE KING
EVEN THE SCORE!"

CHAPTER 6

LIAR ICKY ICK SAYS, "YOU'RE MESSED UP N' DIRTY"

Over time, Lil' J continued to discover the truth, which made Master Deceiver furious. When Lil' J turned eleven, his mom let him start riding the bus home in the afternoon instead of going to the rec center. He hadn't seen Mr. Links in over a year and was starting to feel better.

Seeing Lil's J's spark returning, Master Deceiver decided to send the liar Icky Ick to take Lil' J down for good.

ICKY ICK'S SPECIALTY IS CONVINCING THE KING'S KIDS THEY ARE DIRTY.

Thankfully, the King of Music knew Master Deceiver's wicked plan, so He sent a special friend to help Lil' J fight the next battle.

One day during lunch, a very pretty girl approached Lil' J with a huge grin.

"Hi. I'm Katie. You're in my English class."

Lil' J had seen her on his bus, but hadn't noticed how pretty she was until that moment.

Icky Ick's attack began.

"HI. I'M KATIE. YOU'RE IN MY ENGLISH CLASS."

"HI. I'M LIL' J AND....ERRR... UM...UM..."

LIL' J THOUGHT OF MR. LINKS... THEN HE JUST FELT SLIMY...

ICKY ICK MADE HIM FEEL...

...DIRTY, NASTY...

Just as Lil' J began to say, "Hello," the image of Mr. Links appeared in Lil' J's mind. Tongue-tied, embarrassed, and sick to his stomach, Lil' J heard this nasty beat...

"YO, LITTLE DUDE,
ICKY ICK'S MY NAME.
MAKING YOU SICK,
THAT'LL BE MY FAME.
LIL' J, YOU'RE JUST LIKE ME: USED,
CONFUSED, AND JUST PLAIN NASTY.
IT FELT GOOD, YOU LIKED IT TOO,
NEVER MIND THAT YOU FELT USED.
WHEN YOU WAKE,
I'LL MAKE YOU SLIMY.
WHEN YOU SLEEP
I'LL MAKE YOU GRIMY.
THOUGH YOU HAD NO VOICE TO SAY,
LIL' J, YOU KNOW
YOU LIKED IT THAT WAY."

Lil' J felt so dirty and believed he could never feel clean again. So many thoughts were running through his mind, **WILL I EVER BE NORMAL? WHAT IS NORMAL? DO I WANT TO BE WITH A GIRL NOW OR DO I WANT TO BE WITH A DUDE?**

Lil' J wondered, **WHAT WOULD HAPPEN IF EVERYONE FOUND OUT I DID ALL THOSE**

THINGS WITH MR. LINKS? IF IT FELT GOOD, I MUST HAVE LIKED IT. MY FRIENDS WILL NEVER TALK TO ME AGAIN, AND MY MOM WILL BE SO UPSET WITH ME.

Lil' J knew another secret: that he had dreams at night and sometimes his body responded. He knew he liked the feeling and sometimes he even had thoughts about touching others in their private areas.

Lil' J could never tell anyone about his thoughts and feelings. He was afraid they'd probably put him in jail or something. Master Deceiver was pleased to see

Lil' J's pain and his determination to keep secrets!

    Good news - the King of Music knew Lil' J's feelings were normal, especially after the wrong things Mr. Links did. The King is very angry with Mr. Links, but had a plan to help Lil' J heal and get his music back. Imagine Lil' J's surprise when he heard the voice of the King's other helper, Jazzy Jazz, over the school's intercom!

"YOU'RE BRAVE AND YOU'RE COOL,
YOU WERE JUST
FOLLOWIN' HIS RULE.
YOUR BODY DID JUST FINE;
IT REACTED AS DESIGNED.
YOU SURVIVED N' BRIGHT YOU SHINE;
YOU WON'T BE LEFT BEHIND.
YOU'RE GOOD N' YOU'RE CLEAN,
AN AMAZING FIGHTIN' MACHINE.

YOU'LL WIN THIS WAR;

JUST TOSS THE LIES
RIGHT OUT THE DOOR.
YOUR LIFE'LL BE GREAT;
THERE'S SO MUCH
TO CELEBRATE.
HAVE FAITH IN JOURNEY LONG;
AFTER THE BATTLE
WILL BE YOUR SONG."

Jazzy Jazz entered the lunchroom on a clean-up mission! He grabbed a mop dripping with soapy water to help Lil' J fight this liar!

He said, "Icky Ick has been tellin' you some messed up lies, Lil' J. You are stronger than you think and you can heal. You must fight the lies you're hearing in your

mind. It seems like your own thoughts, but what you hear are lies."

Lil' J began thinking,

"STRONG WARRIOR, WHAT A JOKE!
I'D FIGHT LIKE OLD PEOPLE
AFTER A STROKE.
BETRAYED BY MY BODY,
CAN'T THEY SEE?
MY BODY'S ACTUALLY THE ENEMY.
COULD MY BODY BE 'JUST FINE'?
COULD MY FEELINGS
BE AS DESIGNED?
YOU MAY BE RIGHT, I JUST DON'T KNOW.
HARD TO BELIEVE,
JUST CUZ YOU SAY SO.
I FEEL NASTY, BUT I WANT TO BELIEVE.
I FEEL GROSS,
BUT HAVE I BEEN DECEIVED?"

Jazzy Jazz said, "Lil' J, it's natural to be embarrassed and confused about what Mr. Links did to you, but you need to talk about it to learn the truth. You are brave and can face this just as a strong soldier would do in battle, and then you will be free of it.

Master Deceiver thinks you won't be courageous enough to face the memories, explain your thoughts, and explore your feelings."

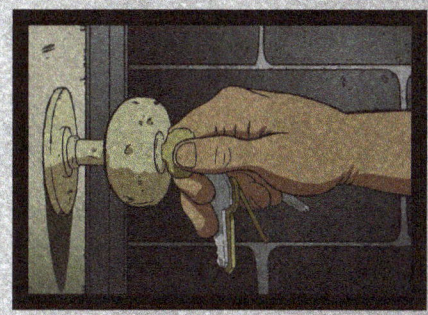

"But...," said Lil' J, putting his head down as the memories and guilt came up. The pain seemed so unbearable that he thought he might vomit!

And this is exactly what Icky Ick wanted. He grinned and tried to slop mud and filth all over Lil' J, but Jazzy Jazz stopped him with a quick sweep of the mop and sent him sliding on the cafeteria floor.

"Listen to me very carefully Lil' J," said Jazzy Jazz. "The truth is your body is amazing and smart. The King made our bodies to automatically feel lots of things like

hot, cold, and ticklish. Your skin detectors keep you safe. For example, if your hand gets near a stove, you immediately pull away. Your brain sends a message,

'Hey, this is really hot, pull away NOW!' Just because your skin said, 'This feels good' instead of 'ouch,' does not mean you're bad or dirty. It just means your skin is doing its job."

Jazzy Jazz continued,

"THE KING CREATED US TO FEEL PLEASURE TOO. OUR BODY DOESN'T KNOW THE DIFFERENCE BETWEEN A SAFE PERSON TOUCHING IT OR SOMEONE ABUSIVE LIKE MR. LINKS. YOU DIDN'T DO ANYTHING WRONG, AND THE GOOD FEELINGS ARE NOT YOUR FAULT. THE KING MADE IT THAT WAY TO PROTECT YOU, AND IT'S GOOD."

Lil' J knew Jazzy Jazz was right and this made Icky Ick angry. He came at Lil' J with all his might, but Lil' J was ready and sprayed Icky Ick right in his slimy face. Lil' J declared,

"THE TRUTH IS I AM NOT DIRTY! I'M WASHING THESE UGLY ATTACKS RIGHT DOWN THE DRAIN! I DIDN'T DO ANYTHING WRONG AND THE GOOD FEELINGS ARE NORMAL.

ICKY ICK GET OUT MY SIGHT;
BETTER RUN CUZ HARD I'LL FIGHT.
NOW I KNOW AND WILL BELIEVE;
CUTTIN' YOU OFF CUZ YOU DECEIVE.
I'LL TELL MY STORY,
DESCRIBE MY FEARS;
LET IT OUT, BE PROUD OF TEARS.
FACING FEELINGS MEANS I'M STRONG;
NOW I KNOW I WASN'T WRONG.
LETTING GO OF HATE AND SHAME,
CHOOSING TO HEAL AND LOSE THE PAIN,
I'M DOIN' GREAT AND SAYIN' LOUD,
WORKIN' HARD AND FEELIN' PROUD.
YOU'RE THE ONE WITH PANTS SO SOILED;
GIG IS UP; YOUR PLAN'S BEEN FOILED.
I'LL MOP YOU UP WITH SPIC-N-SPAN;
SHAKE YOU OFF WITH MY CLEAN HANDS.

CHAPTER 7

CON THE ARTIST SAYS, "YOU'VE GOT A RIGHT TO RAGE!"

It was field day and Lil' J was so excited, mostly because Katie would be there and watching. They had been passing

notes and talking in the hallway for some time. Lil' J signed up for the relay race, tug-a-war, and discus throw. He knew he had a good chance of winning.

Sadly, the day would not go as Lil' J had planned. The boys were at the starting line for the relay race, and Lil' J was focused. That was until he heard Lucas, one of his classmates behind him, say,

"LIL' J'S A WIMP, AND KATIE IS ABOUT TO FIND THAT OUT!"

When Lil' J heard the word "wimp," his face turned red, his temper began to boil, and he totally lost it. Without taking time to think, Lil' J's hand became a fist, and he turned to hit Lucas as hard as possible.

What Lil' J didn't know was that Master Deceiver sent Con the Artist, one of his best liars to field day. Con had been a pro at deceiving people from the beginning of time.

Thankfully, the King of Music was never too far away.

"I DON'T CARE! I'LL SHOW LUCAS WHO'S TOUGH!"
"SSSS...
SSSS...

CON
SSSS...
SSSS... C'MON... HIT. HURT. RAGE."

To fight this liar, the King sent both DJ Rap-a-Lot and Jazzy Jazz to intercept the blow. DJ tried to calm Lil' J down, but Lil' J was too angry and wasn't listening. DJ and Jazzy Jazz knew that if Lil' J did not get his anger under control soon, his life would begin to go down a very dark road.

Con was already wrapping around his heart, her power so strong it took Lil' J's breath away. She whispered in his ear,

"LIL' J, GO FIGHT AND RAGE;
LOCK YOU UP, LION IN A CAGE.
LIL' J, DON'T SNITCH OR TELL,
JUST GO HIT, STEAL,
CHEAT, AND YELL.
FEELINGS, YOU GO CUT THEM OFF;
THE WORLD WILL THINK,
YEA, HE'S GONE SOFT.
IT'S FUN TO CURSE
AND TELL THOSE LIES,

> AUTHORITY ALWAYS TO DEFY.
> GO HURT OTHERS,
> SOMEONE HURT YOU:
> HE STOLE YOUR RAP,
> NO ONE TO SUE.
> OH, THOSE SECRETS YOU WILL KEEP;
> SHAME IS RUNNING, WAY TOO DEEP.
> HATE IS RIGHT, DON'T TELL A SOUL;
> MAJOR JAIL TIME IS MY GOAL."

Con rose up, piercing Lil' J's eyes with her own evil stare; she was going for the kill. But DJ Rap-a-Lot stepped in between and knocked the monster back to the ground.

> "LISTEN TO ME, MY LIL' MAN,
> THERE'S SO MANY THINGS
> YOU DON'T UNDERSTAND.

Time seemed to stand still when Lil' J heard DJ's rhyme. As he stared out at the parents who had come to watch their children on field day, he knew his dad would not be coming. He knew his mom was at work. Lil' J's anger only increased as Con's message, **"GO HURT OTHERS. SOMEONE HURT YOU!"** assaulted Lil' J's mind loud and clear. Lil' J blasted back at DJ Rap-a-Lot,

**"I GOTTA RIGHT TO RAGE
AND JUST TO BE,
NO ONE THERE, HELPING ME.
I HATE MY DAD, I HATE MY MOM;
THEY DON'T CARE,
I LOST MY SONG.
EMPTY NOW, I'LL MAKE THEM PAY;
I'M IN CHARGE,
I'LL RULE MY DAY.**

I WON'T LOVE; I WON'T FEEL; PUNISH ALL, MY FATE IS SEALED."

Jazzy Jazz, with compassion in his heart, spoke out this beat,

"LISTEN AGAIN, LIL' J, IMPORTANT NEWS IN WHAT I SAY!

TRUST ME, YOU'LL WIN THIS WAR;
GOTTA TOSS THOSE LIES
RIGHT OUT THA DOOR.
HOLDING RAGE WON'T SET YOU FREE;
GRANTING THEIR PARDON
WILL BE YOUR KEY.
WASN'T RIGHT, YEAH,
THEY DID YOU WRONG,
BUT FIGHTING BACK
STEALS YOUR SONG.
LET THE KING
SEAL THEIR FATE;
LOOK AROUND,
SEE DESTRUCTION
OF HATE.
SWORD AND WEAPON,
IT'S YOUR SONG;
THE PAIN AND RAGE ONE
DAY BE GONE."

"DON'T LISTEN, LIL' J!"

Lil' J felt his anger subsiding. He realized that Jazzy Jazz was right! Con wanted anger to control Lil' J knowing it would eventually destroy his life.

After Lil' J listened to the opposing sides, he thought it was fitting that his next event was called, tug of war. During the last few years, Lil' J felt as if there was a war going on in his mind.

Lil' J pulled hard at the event, harder than ever before and their team won. Though there would be many difficult battles in Lil' J's life, the King of Music always sent helpers, such as Mrs. Witkin and his friend Katie to help him fight the enemies' lies.

CHAPTER 8

LIL' J PUTS IT ALL TOGETHER

Lil' J had a blast when his team defeated the other team during the tug of war. He especially loved the look he got from Katie when the other team went down.

Katie cared about Lil' J a great deal. She noticed there were times when Lil' J got angry very quickly, but for the most part, he was considerate, smart, and totally funny! Lil' J was thankful that she would remind him to cool off when he was mad, or to study longer when he made a C. For the first time in his life, he felt hopeful.

Lil' J had so much on his mind while he and Katie walked across the field to the last event, the discus throw. He thought about the horrified look on Katie's face when he almost decked Lucas, and about the lessons he'd learned from DJ Rap-a-Lot and Jazzy Jazz over the last few years.

THE MOST IMPORTANT LESSON IS THAT OUR FEELINGS ARE IMPORTANT AND GIVE US CLUES ABOUT WHAT IS GOING ON INSIDE AND IN THE WORLD AROUND US. LETTING OUR FEELINGS CONTROL OUR MIND AND ACTIONS WILL ONLY LEAD TO DISASTER AND MUCH WORSE PAIN!

Lil' J also thought about the day he took a risk and told Mrs. Witkin about Mr. Links touching him. On that very important day, Lil' J discovered he had believed so many lies. First, telling the secret felt like a gazillion pounds of books falling out of his backpack.

Next, when he told his mom, she didn't fall apart as he suspected, but instead helped him talk to the police. Another surprise was that no one was mad or blamed him. This was shocking. Lastly, everyone believed Lil' J, and he was not the one who got in trouble!

TELLING THE SECRET FELT LIKE A GAZILLION POUNDS OF BOOKS FALLING OUT OF HIS BACKPACK.

After about eight months of meeting with a counselor named Dr. Wagner, Lil' J began to understand that it was much easier to stuff the memories and feelings inside, but if he wanted to shine, he needed to be brave enough to face his pain, learn the truth, and then choose to believe it!

As Lil' J stepped into the discus ring, he had flashbacks of the four battles he had won in the last few years. He thought about how far he had come regarding his ability to fight the shame, anger, guilt, and other painful emotions related to the trauma in his life.

Lil' J decided to thank the King of Music for helping him. He determined never to allow negativity to rule his life.

DJ said, "Do you remember the colored stones on each of the Lie Monsters? Those colors reflect the power you were giving Master Deceiver by believing his lies. The King of Music has a motto: 'Once you know the truth, it will set you free.' The King of Music has given you His royal authority to take the power back that the monsters stole from you!"

DJ Rap-a-Lot handed him the disc. Lil' J felt a power surge that was unlike anything he had ever experienced. Lil' J spun around and threw the disc

beyond the realms of space and time.

As the disc passed by each Lie Monster, the colored stone broke loose, and the power the Lie Monster had stolen was absorbed into the disc. The colors of truth swirled all around Lil' J. Suddenly he realized:

**INSTEAD OF SHAME,
HE FELT CONFIDENT,
BRAVE, AND LOVED.**

➤

**INSTEAD OF GUILT,
HE EXPERIENCED
A SENSE OF INNOCENCE AND
PLAYFULNESS.**

➤

**INSTEAD OF FEELING DIRTY,
HE FELT HIS FRESH NEW SONG.**

➤

**INSTEAD OF FEELING RAGE,
HE ACKNOWLEDGED HIS ROYALTY!**

That's when it happened. The colors absorbed everything around them, even the red in Lil' J's hat! They became a blaze of gold fire and formed the letters, T...R...U...T...H right onto his special cap.

Though Lil' J made great progress that day, a warrior must be on guard at all times by reminding himself of the truth. Even though the Lie Monsters can be defeated at each battle, they aren't dead yet. They will make sneak attacks to steal our music and change our rhyme.

When this happens, it's the greatest tragedy ever. Thankfully, the King of Music will never stop sending helpers because He loves our song and He loves our shine!

I AM

©2016 Tammy Kennedy, written and performed by Enlitement.

I was born to shine bright cuz I'm here for a reason.
I'm living proof that it's truth that I'm speaking.
I'm telling you now that right now is my season.
I have no fear; I have no fear. I'm standing right here I'm not leaving.
Watch me as I blast off ever since I took my mask off;
Chains gone, I remain strong. Now watch me get my dance on.
Happy cuz I made it. My life I wouldn't trade it.
If you ain't got nothing nice to say
Then shhhhh; you can save it
Cuz all I do is speak truth, seek truth, teach truth.
I stopped believing those lies, that's what got me through.
I used to feel so down, but now I sit up high
Cuz I am V I C T O R Y

Sticks and stones may break my bones, but your words cannot hurt me
Cuz I know who I am and my foundation's very sturdy.
See back in my past they used to point and laugh,
But now I'm in my future, I say look at my dab.
Get in there, get in there. I was so use to being under
Back then I wouldn't come over, but now I'm an overcomer.
I was feeling so ashamed, had no one I could cry to.
Then that's when the truth came and said I'm here to guide you.
No matter what you say it will not offend
Cuz I'm gonna win, I'm gonna win, I'm gonna win, I'm gonna win.

I AM - Victorious
I AM - A Champion
I AM - Triumphant
I AM - An Overcomer

King's treasure box MINISTRIES®

UNIQUE, INTERACTIVE RESOURCES HELPING GIRLS AND BOYS

HEAL

"We design high-quality therapeutic resources to help children heal after sexual abuse. Our interactive tools will allow you to join them on an adventure as they face their memories, defeat Lie Monsters, and discover a secret...their true identity as royalty."
—Tammy Kennedy, MS *Survivor, Therapist, Author and Speaker*

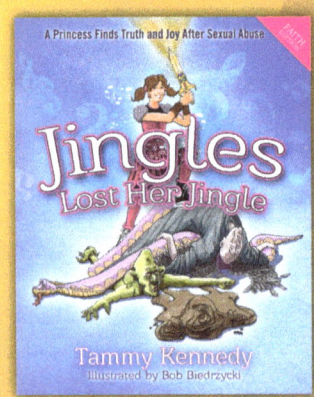

Jingles Lost Her Jingle
General & Faith Editions
Girls 7-12

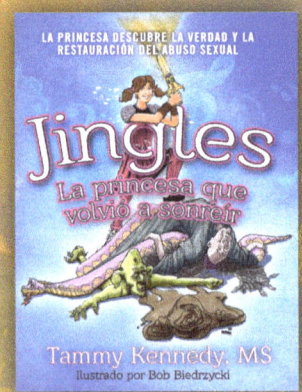

Jingles La Princesa que volvió a sonreír
Spanish Edition

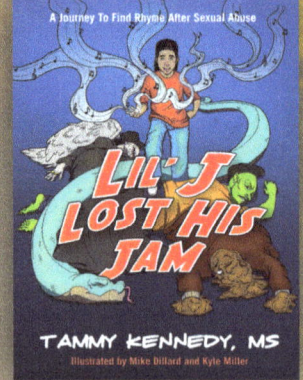

Lil' J Lost His Jam
Boys 7-12

Please join us to help survivors heal. Visit:
KingsTreasureBox.org

The King's Treasure Box Ministries (KTBM) is a 501 (C)3 non-profit, tax-exempt organization. Contributions are tax deductible as allowed by law.

www.ingramcontent.com/pod-product-compliance
Lightning Source LLC
Chambersburg PA
CBHW051549220426
43671CB00022B/2983